FOOTBALL LEGENDS

Troy Aikman

Terry Bradshaw

Jim Brown

Dan Marino

Joe Montana

Joe Namath

Walter Payton

Jerry Rice

Barry Sanders

Deion Sanders

Emmitt Smith

Steve Young

CHELSEA HOUSE PUBLISHERS

DEION SANDERS

Bruce Chadwick

Introduction by
Chuck Noll

CHELSEA HOUSE PUBLISHERS
New York · Philadelphia

Produced by Daniel Bial and Associates
New York, New York

Picture research by Alan Gottlieb
Cover illustration by Bill Vann

3 5 7 9 8 6 4

Chadwick, Bruce.
    Deion Sanders / Bruce Chadwick
    p. cm.—(Football legends)
    Includes bibliographical references and index.
    ISBN 0-7910-2460-1
    1. Sanders, Deion—Juvenile literature. 2. Football players—
United States—Biography—Juvenile literature. 3. Baseball
players—United States—Biography—Juvenile literature.
    [1. Sanders, Deion.   2. Football players. 3. Afro-Americans—
Biography.] I. Title. II. Series.
GV939.S186C43 1996
796.332'092—dc20
    [B]   95-18223
                                                              CIP
                                                               AC

CONTENTS

A WINNING ATTITUDE

Chuck Noll

Don't ever fall into the trap of believing, "I could never do that. And I won't even try—I don't want to embarrass myself." After all, most top athletes had no idea what they could accomplish when they were young. A secret to the success of every star quarterback and sure-handed receiver is that they tried. If they had not tried, if they had not persevered, they would never have discovered how far they could go and how much they could achieve.

You can learn about trying hard and overcoming challenges by being a sports fan. Or you can take part in organized sports at any level, in any capacity. The student messenger at my high school is now president of a university. A reserve ballplayer who got very little playing time in high school now owns a very successful business. Both of them benefited by the lesson of perseverance that sports offers. The main point is that you don't have to be a Hall of Fame athlete to reap the benefits of participating in sports.

In math class, I learned that the whole is equal to the sum of its parts. But that is not always the case when you are dealing with people. Sports has taught me that the whole is either greater than or less than the sum of its parts, depending on how well the parts work together. And how the parts work together depends on how they really understand the concept of teamwork.

Most people believe that teamwork is a fifty-fifty proposition. But true teamwork is seldom, if ever, fifty-fifty. Teamwork is *whatever it takes to get the job done.* There is no time for the measurement of contributions, no time for anything but concentrating on your job.

One year, my Pittsburgh Steelers were playing the Houston Oilers in the Astrodome late in the season, with the division championship on the line. Our offensive line was hard hit by the flu, our starting quarterback was out with an injury, and we were having difficulty making a first down. There was tremendous pressure on our defense to perform well—and they rose to the occasion. If the players on the defensive unit had been measuring their contribution against the offense's contribution, they would have given up and gone home. Instead, with a "whatever it takes" attitude, they increased their level of concentration and performance, forced turnovers, and got the ball into field goal range for our offense. Thanks to our defense's winning attitude, we came away with a victory.

Believing in doing whatever it takes to get the job done is what separates a successful person from someone who is not as successful. Nobody can give you this winning outlook; you have to develop it. And I know from experience that it can be learned and developed on the playing field.

My favorite people on the football field have always been offensive linemen and defensive backs. I say this because it takes special people to perform well in jobs in which there is little public recognition when they are doing things right but are thrust into the spotlight as soon as they make a mistake. That is exactly what happens to a lineman whose man sacks the quarterback or a defensive back who lets his receiver catch a touchdown pass. They know the importance of being part of a group that believes in teamwork and does not point fingers at one another.

Sports can be a learning situation as much as it can be fun. And that's why I say, "Get involved. Participate."

CHUCK NOLL, the Pittsburgh Steelers head coach from 1969–1991, led his team to four Super Bowl victories—the most by any coach. Widely respected as an innovator on both offense and defense, Noll was inducted into the Pro Football Hall of Fame in 1993.

1

THE LONGEST DAY

At 3:53 A.M., October 11, 1992, while the sun was still struggling to peep over the horizon, shrimp-boat crews below were waking up for early morning work, and children all over Florida were still asleep, Deion Sanders, his eyes barely open, peered out the window of his Canadair jet as it started to approach the runway of Fort Lauderdale Hollywood Airport. He would soon head for the Atlanta Falcons' team hotel to grab a quick five hours of sleep and then go to Joe Robbie Stadium, in Miami, where he would start at defensive back when the Falcons played the Miami Dolphins. The day before, Sanders practiced baseball in Pittsburgh with his other sports team, the Atlanta Braves, who were playing the Pittsburgh Pirates in the playoffs for the National League pennant.

En route to a 1992 playoff baseball game, Deion Sanders exits the helicopter that has brought him to Pittsburgh. Earlier in the day, he had played football in Miami (which explains why he is wearing shorts while the temperature is in the 50s).

Sanders would rush to another airport when the Falcons' game ended, get on another jet, and fly back to Pittsburgh by 8:30 P.M. when the next game in the baseball playoffs started. It was the first time an athlete played games in two different pro sports on the same day.

It was yet another first for "Neon" Deion Sanders. In just a few short years, two-sport-star Deion Sanders had become one of the most famous and talked about athletes in the world. He had a variety of nicknames that he liked to use which many children used as their own. He produced and starred in rap-music videos and would soon go on a national musical tour. He wore large sunglasses like movie stars, underwear with dollar signs on them, and, at the start of his career, he always had several gold chains draped around his neck, one with the number 21—his football jersey number. He wore lots of rings. He was a nonstop talker whose favorite subject was himself. He was a show-off, talking trash to opposing players, putting his hands behind his helmet as he crossed the goal line, high stepping his way up the field with interceptions and kickoffs. Sometimes he wound up in the headlines for the wrong reasons : an on-field fight with football receiver Andre Rison, a scuffle with a Cincinnati security guard, dumping ice water on a television commentator, wars with the media, contract arguments. But he was one of the best athletes in the United States. Today, though, would be his longest day, perhaps the longest day in sports history.

Sanders, who also nicknamed himself "Prime Time," boarded the team bus at the hotel at 10:47 A.M., clearly still tired, and rode with his football teammates to the stadium, where he

In his afternoon game, Sanders shut down Mark (Super) Duper.

worked out for an hour before the game. His coach told him he would return punts and kick-offs, start at defensive back, and perhaps get in as a wide receiver, even though the baseball playoffs prevented him from practicing with the Falcons during the week.

At precisely 1:01 P.M. the Dolphins kicked off and Sanders drifted back into the middle of the end zone to catch the ball, which he downed for a touchback. Nine minutes later, after the Falcon offense stalled, Sanders went in as a defensive back. It was a good game for Deion, even though he did not intercept any passes or score any touchdowns. He returned one punt for

Sanders pinch-hits in Game 4 of the 1992 playoffs.

short yardage and ran back two kickoffs for 23 and 19 yards. Just after the beginning of the second period he caught a nine-yard pass on offense. Most importantly, he smothered receivers as a defensive back, preventing numerous first downs. The Dolphins had two of the best wide receivers in the National Football League—Mark Clayton and Mark "Super" Duper—and Deion held them each in check.

The Falcon offense played well, running up a 17–7 lead going into the final quarter. But the Dolphins were the better team. They scored two touchdowns in the last period to win, 21–17.

Deion Sanders, like the other Falcons, walked off the field with his head down. He did not have much time for sadness, though, because now he had to race to the airport in order to fly back to Pittsburgh to play in the National League Championship Series. He did not feel well, either. A quick shower did not help and he reported to a doctor. A pro football game takes a lot out of a player at any time, but Deion had played baseball all week and spent three hours in the air before this game. He was tired. The doctors, knowing Deion still had a long day ahead of him, gave him two intravenous treatments to pick up his energy.

One thing Deion Sanders always had plenty of was energy. It was that remarkable energy which had brought him to this day, a day in which he would make sports history. It was his energy which made him a three-sport star in high school and an All-American at Florida State University. It was his energy which made him a first-round draft pick in baseball by the New York Yankees in 1988 and a first-round pick by the football Falcons that same year—a rare double pick. It was energy which got him through a baseball season with the Yankees in the spring and summer of 1989 and then a full football season with the Falcons in the fall of that year. It was energy, and enormous talent, which helped him hit .304 for the Braves in that championship season of 1992, after starting off the year hitting over .400 for nearly a month. He was just as good at football, averaging five interceptions a year and averaging nearly 10 yards per punt return and 23 yards per kickoff return. It was his high level of energy, and an inner faith in himself, which made him the only player since Bo Jackson strong enough and talented enough to not merely play two pro sports but star in each.

Now it was time for the second half of Deion's remarkable pro sports doubleheader—the baseball game. Time was running out for him, though, so instead of a limousine, he took a private helicopter to the airport, lifting off from the parking lot of the stadium at 5:02 P.M. with only twenty minutes to make his flight.

The helicopter landed a minute late at Opa-locka Airport, coming down within sight of the plane, which was on strict orders to wait for its special passenger. Deion jumped out of the helicopter and ran to the plane, which took off for Pittsburgh immediately. Sanders, who had no lunch, wolfed down a quick meal on the plane and tried to take a short nap, with little success, as the plane hurtled over the Carolinas toward Pennsylvania.

Not everybody thought playing two sports on the same day was a good idea. Deion was criticized for it in many newspapers. Tim McCarver, one of the television commentators for the baseball playoffs, was extremely critical. He said it was "flat out wrong" for Sanders to play football and baseball in one day, that he would be dead tired for the baseball game and that he had promised the Braves he would play baseball full time. Terence Moore, a sportswriter for the Atlanta *Constitution*, Deion's hometown paper, said that Deion was not being loyal to the Braves by playing football.

Others thought it was a good idea. The people whose opinions Deion valued most were his teammates, and they backed him up.

"He is a tremendous guy to have around because he gives us an attitude we seem to lack without him," said Falcons cornerback Tim McKyer.

Falcons' center Jamie Dukes also supported Deion. "I wouldn't want to play without him. I think most guys here agree," he said.

His football coach, Jerry Glanville, also agreed. "Everyone notices his athletic ability. Everyone notices his God-given talent. But what's inside of him, how much he cares about people, is even bigger," the coach said.

Deion stuck to his guns. "Everybody said 'this is great—go do it.' This is the sort of thing kids dream about. In the morning, they're Michael Jordan on the basketball court and in the afternoon they're Deion Sanders on the football field. I'm a kid still," he said.

The plane touched down at Allegheny County Airport, near Pittsburgh, at 7:45 P.M., just one hour before the start of Game Five of the baseball playoffs (the Braves would win the pennant in game seven and go on to the World Series). Darkness was falling. Sanders jumped into a waiting helicopter, part of an elaborate plan to get him into the dugout on time. Unable to land anywhere near the stadium, the pilot landed on top of the Channel 11 television news building in downtown Pittsburgh. A waiting elevator whisked Deion to the street, where he leaped into a waiting limousine which raced through traffic to Three Rivers Stadium. Deion got to the stadium at 8:28 P.M., ran from the limo to the locker room, quickly changed into his baseball uniform and ran to the dugout, his cleats banging on the cement floors of the hallway, just as the orchestra started to play the national anthem and the overflow crowd started to stand up. He made it! The Pirates won the game 7–1 as Barry Bonds broke out of his playoff slump. Atlanta's coach Bobby Cox kept Deion on the bench in case he was needed for pinch-running or pinch-hitting late in the game, but the Braves never mounted much of a threat. Still, Deion was ready, and supported his teammates from the bench.

2

THE KID WHO WAS TOO SMALL

Everybody at North Fort Myers High School knew who Deion Sanders was the very first day he stepped through the front doors of the school. He made an impression right away, as he always did, but it was the wrong impression.

It was lunchtime on a hot August day in Florida. Deion and his new high school friends finished their meals in the school cafeteria when Deion spotted a wooden crate filled with pint cartons of milk, the kind most schools serve. His eyes wide and his eyebrows tilted, he motioned to his friends and quietly walked over to the crate. He swooped up half a dozen cartons of milk and walked out the door of the cafeteria, his friends walking slightly behind him, and began to eye the roof of the high school. He told his friends he was going to heave the milk onto the roof of the school. They told him he would get into trouble. He heaved them up to the roof anyway.

In high school, Deion Sanders was a star baseball, basketball, and football player.

Deion was a left-handed quarterback before he was switched to defense.

A teacher saw Deion toss the cartons and ordered him to report to the high school principal. The freshman did and was told by the principal that the punishment for something like that was paddling with a wooden paddle (that punishment is no longer permitted in the state of Florida). Deion told him that there was no way he would be paddled. The principal called his mother, Connie Knight, and explained what Deion did and that he refused to be paddled.

"You go right ahead and paddle him!" said his mother.

That was the first and last time anyone had to paddle Deion Sanders.

The legend that has grown around Deion Sanders is inaccurate, as most sports legends are. Deion was not a great athlete when he arrived at North Fort Myers High School, bused there each day from a black section of Fort Myers where he lived. He was certainly a good athlete. As a boy in public grade school, he played Little League baseball, playground basketball, and Pop Warner football. His football team was one of the best in the country, but Deion was not one of the better players. He was too small.

"Very small. I'll bet he did not weigh 125 pounds when he got here. He was a tall, skinny kid," said Ron Hoover, Deion's high school football coach.

Deion, an average student, wanted to play high school sports more than any other student Hoover ever met, though, and coaches let him. He was different than most schoolboy athletes.

"When he was in high school, I don't think he ever had it in his mind to be in the NFL or play major league baseball or anything like that. I'm not even sure he saw himself playing college sports. What everybody loved about Deion was that he played sports for the sheer love it, for the thrill of it. That kid loved every minute he was on a basketball court or football field. He just loved it. He truly played it just for fun and he had a good time. People loved to watch him play because when he was having fun, everybody was having fun," said Barbara "Bobbie" Dewey, the school's athletic director, who has known Deion for years. "He was just a joy to watch."

At North Fort Myers, Deion quickly became a starter, but not a star, for the baseball team. He became a left-handed quarterback, a very light quarterback, for the football team. He played at point guard for the basketball team. Basketball was easily his best sport in high school.

"He was incredible at basketball, just incredible," said Mrs. Dewey. "Just before games, to entertain people, he'd stand flat-footed under the basket with a ball in each hand, then leap up into the air and dunk both balls, one right after the other, like he was hanging in the air, defying gravity. The fans would just go nuts when he did that."

Everybody thought basketball was Deion's future. "He had amazing vision on the court. He knew where everybody was every moment of the game. He had a sixth sense. He had a good jump shot and had an amazing leap to grab rebounds. He was very quick on defense. His best sport was definitely basketball. If he wanted to, he could play in the NBA right now," said Mrs. Dewey.

There was no talk of pro sports during Deion's high school days, though, because of his weight and height. As a sophomore, he was about 5'8" and just 125 pounds. He was too small, too light, and he did not have the total dedication he later developed in college. "Don't get me wrong," said one of his high school coaches. "He did not goof off. He just was not intense. He played for the fun of it."

Sometimes he had too much fun. In his senior year, when he was team leader in football, Deion got into an argument with one of his gym teachers and started yelling at him. This time the teacher did not go to the principal but to the football coach. Deion, the best player on the team, was benched for a game as punishment. He never talked back to a teacher again.

Those two incidents (the gym teacher and the milk cartons) were the only two blemishes on Deion's high school record. Many writers today seem to think Deion was always a problem kid, but teachers and neighbors who knew him will deny that. It is just a media myth. Deion was never a problem student. In fact, Sanders, who wore an easy smile most days, was one of the best-liked students at North Fort Myers High by students and teachers alike.

Like everyone, Deion had heroes as a boy.

His biggest hero was boxer Muhammad Ali. His favorite baseball player was Hank Aaron, the man who broke Babe Ruth's home run record. In basketball, he admired Julius Erving

"He was very easy going and got along with everybody. He was never involved in any sort of rivalry with another boy over a girl, never hung out with kids who were in trouble or gave people a hard time. People liked to be around him," said one of his teachers.

Sanders's biggest fan during his high school sports days was his mother, Connie. She and Deion's natural father were divorced when Deion was young and she raised Deion by herself. It was never easy. To make ends meet, Connie Knight always held down at least two jobs, sometimes even three. She worked hard all day and sometimes at night to pay the rent and buy food. Yet, despite the time she spent at work, she was home often for her son.

"I have never known a mother and son to have that close a relationship, that loving a relationship. Everything that Deion did, he did for his mom. He was totally devoted to her," said a friend.

It was his mother, people said, who encouraged Deion to use his ability at sports to win a scholarship to college and his mother, more than anyone else, who convinced him that through hard work he could become a much better athlete than he was in high school. She had a vision of his future that no one else did, not even Deion.

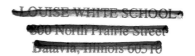

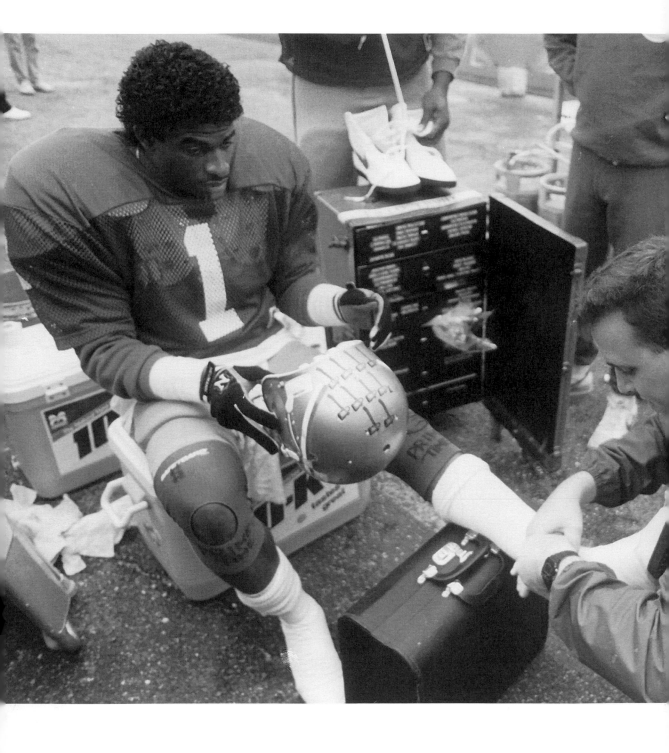

3

ALL-AMERICAN

Many great college and pro stars were standout players as children, stars of their Little League, Pop Warner, and high school teams and were recruited by colleges. Many were not. For every star who had 100 college scholarship offers, there were stars who were not heavily recruited in high school. They were the diamonds in the rough.

Some great college and pro stars did not even play football until they were teenagers and earned starting jobs on college teams as "walkons"—nonscholarship players who turned out, unannounced, for the team. Many later stars were seen by scouts while in high school but written off as "too slow," "not heavy enough," or having "bad hands" or "no defense."

Deion Sanders was almost one of them.

Deion was a left-handed quarterback. His high school coaches were happy to have such a superb athlete run the offense. But college coaches were in no hurry to sign a lefty—their

Deion, who usually wore the number 2, started to gain a fair amount of attention when he played for Florida State.

offenses were set up to be run by a righty. Besides, while Deion had been good in the games he started for North Fort Myers, he had not been outstanding.

Deion was so underrated as a quarterback that Florida State University did not want to recruit him for football. FSU was famed for making stars out of little-known local products, and in the mid-1980s they had one of college football's top teams. They had made up their mind they were not interested in Deion.

Mickey Andrews, Florida State's defensive coach, who turned the Seminoles defense into one of the most fearsome in America, smiles as he leans back in his leather chair at Doak Campbell Stadium, in Tallahassee, Florida, and talks about Deion. A cluster of palm trees sways in the wind outside his window.

"We had seen his game films and passed on him as a football quarterback. He was left-handed, he was basically a running quarterback, not a drop-back passer, and just did notfit into our program at all. I never thought he could make it anywhere as a quarterback. Later, in the middle of the winter, I went to his high school for a banquet or something and a coach took me to see the high school basketball game. Deion was the star of the team. I think Deion played 16 different sports in high school," laughed Andrews. "I just couldn't believe how good Deion was at movement. He was a sensational shooter and a good defensive player, but what absolutely amazed me was his ability to stop and go, to turn and to move without the ball. He could back pedal down the court to cover on a fast break faster than most men could run forward. He had great peripheral vision, could see everybody moving on the court, and had a great sense of what was going to happen. He'd pick off passes, move to the basket, do everything a second ahead of everybody else. I've never seen anyone who could leap like Deion. He was a great basketball player. I'm sitting there on these wood benches in the stands and I tell myself I'm not seeing a kid play basketball, I'm seeing a kid play defensive back in football. He had all the moves of a great defensive back. All of them. Later I learned how fast he was for kickoffs and punt returns. We met a bit later and we eventually talked him into going to Florida State."

At Florida State, Sanders worked hard at learning how to become a good defensive back. It was difficult because Florida State used one of the most sophisticated defensive systems in the country. By his sophomore year, Deion had become a starter. He fit right in. More than anything else, it was his speed that made him great.

"If he had any problems covering a man, or cutting the way his man cut or reading the play, it was overcome by that amazing speed," said one of his coaches. "In several steps, he'd be all over somebody. Speed was the one thing he had in abundance . . . and still does."

Once he learned how to play defense in the FSU system, Deion became the best defensive back in the country, earning numerous honors, including All-American in 1987 and 1988, and he helped lead the team to records of 9–3 in 1985, 7–4–1 in 1986, 11–1 in 1987, and 11–1 in 1988. While Deion was at FSU, the Seminoles went to the Gator Bowl, All-American Bowl, Fiesta Bowl, and Sugar Bowl. They won all four games. The team was ranked 15th in the nation

Next to Deion Sanders in this gathering of the 1988 AP All-America Football team is Barry Sanders (#21). The man not in uniform is comedian Bob Hope.

in 1985, second in 1987 and third in 1988. Deion served as co-captain for the 1988 season.

Deion intercepted 14 passes in his career at Florida State, three in bowl games, and stunned the entire football world with a 100-yard interception against Tulsa University as a freshman. But Sanders was never "just" a defensive back, just as he was never "just" a football player. He also ran back kickoffs and punt returns, setting school records there, too, including a 76-yard punt return for a touchdown against Clemson University. As a senior, he led the nation in punt returns with a 15.2 yards-per-catch average. His finest moment was the day he turned to the opponents bench and bragged to them that he would run a punt back for a touchdown. He kept pointing up in the air, where the ball would be, and then down toward their end zone. The players laughed at him. Deion then looked up at the Florida State fans behind the players and repeated his shouts and gestures. Sure enough, he caught the ball right in front of the opponents bench, shouted to them that he would score, and he did.

"Neon Deion" was not born until the middle of Sanders's senior year. Until then, the Deion everyone knew wore no gold chains, made no music videos, did no dance steps, had no nickname, and made no efforts to draw attention to himself. Attention is what he got, though, from his coaches, fans, and the media. He earned it for his talent and his work ethic.

"Today, everybody talks about Deion's jewelry and his nicknames and things like that, but here at Florida State we knew him as a very well balanced individual who was generous to other students. He was a good kid from a good home, very attached to his mother. He listened to everything coaches told him, was open to all suggestions and studied football like it was a science. He was not only one of the best football players I ever coached, but one of those I really admired for his determination to practice," said Florida State coach Bobby Bowden. "If any kid who's struggling hard to make a team, any team, wants to know how he has to practice in order to be good, there's no one better to take a look at than Deion Sanders."

Defensive coach Andrews agreed. "I can't remember anyone who worked harder than Deion. You always hear that saying, 'he was the first player on the field for practice and the last one off it.' Well, Deion was the first on, the last off and then back on it again to try out one more move. He worked himself hard. He also became one of the most improved players on our team. He was not All America when he got here. He was not a great player. He was a good player. He knew that. Sanders was not satisfied with being good. He insisted that he could be great, knew the road to that was hard work and followed that road. Most players don't do that," said Andrews. "More than any other player I have coached or even seen, Deion Sanders made himself an All American, made himself great."

But after the hard work and the records, it

was time for something else—"Prime Time."

Coach Bowden remembered the transformation. Sitting on his living room couch in shorts and a flowery shirt, Bowden puts his right foot up on a coffee table and folds his hands in front of him as he talks about Sanders.

"It was about mid-season in his senior year. I don't remember which game. We won it, though. I was in the locker room walking around and the reporters were going from player to player, as they always do, and they get to Deion. In the previous three years, Deion would dutifully answer questions and that would be it. No big deal. I'm standing there watching and all of a sudden he transformed himself into 'Prime Time.' He was like a totally different person. He started telling the press he was 'Prime Time' Sanders. Later it became 'Neon Deion.' I think he had just started talking to a guy who later became his agent, or maybe someone else, and they convinced him he needed a new personality. And there it was—'Prime Time.'

"Actually, since I liked Deion so much as a person, I thought it was kind of funny. For him, it was a very good idea. It made him something special and probably made him a millionaire. I don't think anyone who knows him resents that big transformation—for the media and the public—because they know that underneath the real Deion is still the same—good man, good father, hard worker," said Bowden.

Neon Deion did not merely light up Doak Campbell Stadium. He shone across the street at Dick Howser Stadium, too, where the Seminole baseball team played. There, Sanders worked just as hard as he did at football, winning a starting spot on the team and going on to become one of the best baseball players in the country. The same speed and quickness that made him so good at football made him a superb outfielder. His speed enabled him to cover ground easily in the wide open grassy outfields at Howser Stadium. He ran gracefully, too, with long strides, and was rarely unable to catch up with a line drive.

He had a unique batting stance in college. He drew two lines on the batter's box as soon as he stepped up to the plate. "I'm reminding myself where to plant my back foot and where my front foot should end up when I stride into the pitch," he said. He also had a quick eye.

"He had tremendous hand-eye coordination. As soon as the ball left the pitcher's hand, Deion was moving on it. Most players have to wait a split mini-second. Not him. His hands were ready to swing or hold up right away. He'd follow the ball in and whack it. He was very consistent, too, able to hit all kinds of pitchers. Pitchers were never able to intimidate him. He rarely hit for power, but he could spray hits to all fields," said a Florida State student who watched him play.

His speed also enabled him to become one of the best base stealers in college baseball, and by the time he was ready to graduate major league baseball scouts made Howser Stadium part of their tour. His batting, base stealing, and fielding skills quickly made him one of the best players available in the 1988 draft.

In June of his senior year, Deion was faced with a difficult choice, a choice very few athletes ever had to make—should he play professional football or professional baseball. Or both?

4

TAKE ME OUT TO THE BALLGAME— BOTH OF THEM

Most players dream about being drafted by a major league baseball team. They start dreaming when they are in Little League and the dream grows as they grow. The chances, of course, are slim, less than one in a million. To be drafted, players have to play well in high school and college and show the necessary potential for the major leagues. Thousands of fine college players are ignored in the draft because they lack certain skills.

Being drafted by a National Football League team is just as difficult. There, too, the chances are slender, particularly for defensive backs. Each year, only about 30 defensive backs—out of 9,000 college athletes who play the position— are drafted.

Being drafted by both the major leagues and the NFL is just about impossible, but that is just what happened to Deion Sanders. He was a

As Sanders waited for his name to be called in the 1989 football draft, he already had bought a lot of jewelry and an earring in the shape of a dollar sign.

Sanders quickly became one of pro football's best punt returners. Here he tows Izel Jenkins in a game against the Eagles.

two-time All American at football, and for a top three team, and a natural selection there. He was a superior hitter and base stealer in baseball, and for a championship college baseball team, and a natural selection there, too.

What would he play? Baseball or football?

Deion started to talk about playing both as soon as the New York Yankees drafted him in baseball (he was picked late, in the 30th round, because the Yankees thought he would play professional football) and the Atlanta Falcons named him as their first round pick (number five over all) in football. Impossible? Yes and no.

Several athletes have played two professional sports at the same time. Bo Jackson is probably the most famous because he was a Heisman Trophy winner. Others did what Bo did starting way back with Jim Thorpe, perhaps the greatest athlete who ever lived. Thorpe won the gold medal in the pentathlon at the 1912 Olympics. He played professional baseball for the New York Giants from 1913 to 1919 and then played in the minor leagues in Ohio through the middle of the 1920s. He played professional football as early as 1916 and in the NFL from 1919 to 1925. George Halas, longtime owner of the Chicago Bears, played football with the Chicago Staleys (later the Bears) and baseball with the Yankees in 1919. Jackie Robinson played minor league pro football in the Pacific Coast Football League in 1944 and 1945 and pro baseball with the Kansas City Monarchs in the Negro Leagues at the same time before breaking the color barrier and playing for the Brooklyn Dodgers in 1947. Other same time, two-sport stars were Tommy Brown (Green Bay Packers and Washington Senators), Dave DeBusschere (New York Knicks and Chicago White Sox), Gene Conley (Milwaukee Braves and Boston Celtics), Steve Hamilton (New York Yankees and Minneapolis Lakers, NBA), Ron Reid (Detroit Pistons and Atlanta Braves), Bill Sharman (Boston Celtics and Brooklyn Dodgers minor league), Dick Groat (Pittsburgh Pirates and Fort Wayne, NBA), Otto Graham (Cleveland Browns and Rochester Royals, NBA), Chuck Connors (Brooklyn Dodgers and Rochester Royals, NBA), Del Rice (St. Louis Cardinals and Rochester Royals), Bud Grant (NFL coach and Minneapolis Lakers player), Danny Ainge (Toronto Blue Jays and Boston Celtics), and Chuck Dressen (Chicago Bears and Cincinnati Reds).

It is difficult.

The first problem, of course, is becoming a star in either sport. Thorpe was one of football's greatest players, but he only hit .252 in baseball. DeBusschere was a fine basketball player but an average pitcher (2-4 in two seasons). Ainge is a good basketball player, but only hit .220 in baseball. Dressen was a fine baseball player who hit .272 in eight seasons and went on to a long career as a manager, but he was an average football player. Otto Graham was an outstanding quarterback but a mediocre basketball player. The list goes on. The only athlete to star in football and baseball was Bo Jackson, but a hip injury first cut short his gridiron career. He maintained his baseball career as long as he could, but the injury cut that short, too.

Then along came Deion.

Sanders did not know what he wanted to do in the summer of 1989. He loved to play both sports and could not bring himself to give up one for the other. He struggled at the plate for the Yankees in 1989, hitting just .234 in 14 games after he spent most of the season in the minor leagues, and was often criticized by the press for his gold chains and nonstop talking about himself. He became involved in unhappy contract talks, too, and by the end of 1990, when he hit just .158, he did not want to stay in New York even though he still loved baseball. The Falcons had little trouble convincing him to play defensive back for them in the fall of 1989. They inked him to a four-year deal worth $4.4 million. He got $2 million as an up-front signing bonus; it was the highest signing bonus in NFL history and the highest salary ever paid to a defensive back. "Our feeling when we drafted him was that he was the best overall athlete we'd ever drafted, ever," said Falcons vice president Taylor Smith. "We had a lot to lose if he'd decided to play baseball only."

The problem, then and now, was how to play in both leagues with overlapping seasons. Baseball extended through the end of September and football started at the beginning of September. If any baseball team he played on made the playoffs, it would be even harder to play football. What to do? The Falcons, a struggling team in need of a

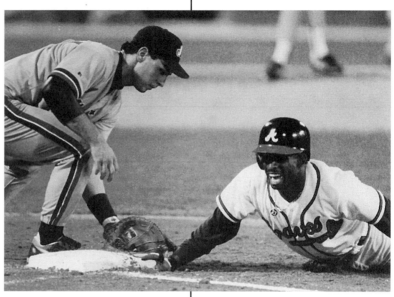

Safe! Montreal's Greg Colbrunn can not get the tag down quickly enough, and Sanders just beats the pick-off attempt.

better secondary, compromised. They agreed to let Deion finish his baseball season and then join the team with little practice. It was the kind of agreement Deion was to have in some form with all of his baseball and football teams.

The 1989 football season was only a few weeks old when Sanders had become a lightning rod of controversy. His new image bothered sportswriters and some fans. He is a show-off. He wears gold chains and a necklace with a gold "21" (his football number) dangling from it; he drives big, fancy cars (he owns 11, all black—for pride in his race); he wears dark sunglasses, custom-made spikes, and wraps a kerchief

Flamboyance has its price. Although Sanders legged out a triple on this hit, he was briefly slowed by the necklace that got caught in his mouth.

around his head when he plays football; he cuts rap-music records and music videos, shows up on Saturday Night Live, and sings with his own group on national music tours; and when he scores touchdowns, he high steps into the end zone, showing off to the crowd. In locker rooms, he plays a rap music song about himself on a cassette recorder—sung by himself.

He told sportswriters that to pump himself up each morning, he asks his bathroom mirror, "Mirror, Mirror, on the wall, who's the fairest of them all?" He then tells the frowning writers that the mirror shouts back at him, "You are, Deion!"

He truly was Neon Deion, the Prime Time star. He flaunted it. He was different, very different, something people had never seen before, and some criticized him for it. Deion, of course, never acted in private as he did in public, as members of his family and close friends knew. "That's all just for entertainment," Deion said of his showboating.

Actually, Deion is a devoted husband to his wife, Carolyn, and their two children. When he received the bonus for signing his first football contract, he bought his mother a house and told her never to work again. He spends every minute off the field with his children. He reads the Bible frequently, is respectful of others, and works hard on all of his teams to improve black/white race relations between players (on the Braves, his best friend was white pitcher Steve Avery).

When he is not with his wife and children, he is out on some lake or river fishing all day with friends. When asked if he had a wild night-life, Deion told reporters he did—he went fishing.

"I want to be a positive person for kids. I went to college. I got an education. I stayed on the straight and narrow. I don't smoke. I don't drink. So the kids looked up to me, an athlete. All the drug dealers were mad because I showed the kids they could get what they have but in a positive way," said Deion, who insists that people look under the glitter to find the real man.

"He is a dedicated family man," said San Francisco 49er lineman Bart Oates. "He runs home as soon as practice is over, is out the door after a Sunday game to meet his wife and hug his kids. He is always talking about his wife and the kids—all the time. Behind all the showbiz glitter, there's a very decent guy."

His showboat style did not bother teammates on the Falcons. In his very first year with them, 1989, Neon Deion had five interceptions, averaged 11 yards per punt return, and 20.7 yards per carry on kickoff returns and even caught passes on his way to making All Pro. He was just as good in 1990, with three interceptions, 21.8 yards per kickoff return, and three touchdowns.

The year 1991 was a turning point. Deion,

fed up with New York, jumped at a chance to play baseball with the Atlanta Braves, his idol Hank Aaron's team. He joined them in spring training, right after football season. It was not a happy baseball year, though. Deion did not hit well and was sent down to the minors. Fed up with baseball, he quit on July 31 and announced that he would only play football.

John Schuerholz, general manager of the Braves, talked him into coming back as the Braves began a pennant drive. "He is one of the most popular guys on the team. He has a positive, upbeat spirit. This kind of baseball situation, when you are battling for a pennant, is very compelling and exciting and Deion senses it as well," said Schuerholz.

Deion, never able to make a clean break from baseball, agreed. "I love these guys. These guys are just like my family," he said, and he returned to the team.

Sanders did not have a good year during the rest of 1991, hitting only .191 for the year, but a boyhood dream came true when he got to play in the World Series with the Braves. The hard-hitting Atlanta team, so dreadful just a few years before, took the Minnesota Twins to the seventh and final game of the World Series before losing.

Deion was caught between his two sports as soon as football practice began, though, and immediately had problems, as he nearly always had. The Falcons would get him for 13 of their 15 regular season games plus any and all play-off games, but he had to practice with the team in August. The Braves would get him for the entire season plus any playoff or World Series games. Meeting that schedule was a problem, as

it always was. He had to fly to Cincinnati with
the Braves to play baseball and then rush back
to Suwanee, Georgia, to practice football with
the Falcons. He did it just like he later did it
during the playoffs of 1992—with fast cars, heli-
copters, and special flights. He practiced football
during the day and played baseball at night.

He had a great year for the Falcons with a
career high 6 interceptions, a 22.2 yard per
kickoff return average, and 2 touchdowns.
Despite limited summer practice, he once again
was acknowledged as one of the game's top
defensive backs and made All Pro again as he
helped the Falcons to one of their best years
ever. The team finished with a 10-6 record in
the regular season, won their first playoff game,
and then lost to the Washington Redskins, who
would go on to win the Super Bowl.

5

CHAMPIONS AT LAST

The Atlanta Braves were the worst team in baseball in 1988 and 1989. The Braves lost a team record 106 games in 1988, finishing dead last in the West Division of the National League, and finished last again in 1989. They were so bad that at baseball card shows $12 Braves tickets were being sold for just $1— and nobody bought them. By the end of 1989, average attendance at Fulton County Stadium had dropped to about 8,000 people per game, less than the turnout for local high school football games.

Major changes took place between 1989 and 1991, however, particularly in pitching additions, and the Braves climbed steadily up the National League ladder and got into the World Series. The spring of 1992 brought hopes that the Braves might make the playoffs again and this time win the World Series. They had strong

Catchers sometimes fear a play at the plate with Deion. Although other baseball players are bigger, Sanders excels at knocking the ball lose—or running over the catcher.

pitching and good hitting and, in the spring, they had a red-hot Deion Sanders. Superstar Otis Nixon sat out the first month of the season on suspension, and Deion replaced him. Neon Deion, completely focused on baseball again (he announced that he was not playing football anymore, as he did just about every spring), was on a tear. He hit safely in 14 consecutive games and then went on to hit .426 for the first month of the season. The Braves soon jumped into first place.

The year 1992 was a turnaround year for Sanders. He changed his batting stance, ending his longtime crouch, and faced pitchers standing almost erect. He changed his attitude on pitchers. He told teammates that as the leadoff hitter he was not taking enough pitches and not drawing enough walks. He started to look at more pitches and not only drew walks—which resulted in steals—but forced hurlers to feed him better pitches, which he drilled into the outfield. He also corrected his swing and made up his mind to hit at least .300.

Numerous injuries complicated that goal. He had a hairline fracture of his left foot when the season started and later jammed a finger stealing a base, forcing him to play for weeks with two fingers taped together.

Mentally, he changed his outlook. "I calm myself down for baseball now," he said. "I'm keeping a book. After every game I write down what they think it takes to get me out, how they come at me, their moves, everything."

Critics thought Deion's fast start would fizzle. After all, Sanders only hit .191 in 1991. How could anyone increase his average by more than 50 percent in a single season? Deion did.

He settled in at about .316 in midseason and hit over .300 right through the end of the year, finishing the year with a solid .304 batting average, one of the tops in the league. He also scored 54 runs and stole 26 bases.

"Deion is aggressive, and that's what makes that team's offense," said Los Angeles Dodger manager Tommy Lasorda. The Braves stayed in first place through the end of the season and wound up in the playoffs again. It was Deion's finest year in baseball and the second great year in a row for the Braves. Deion had finally proved to himself, the writers, and the fans that he could play baseball with the best of them.

Naturally, as the summer wore on, Deion started to think about football once again. He could not get his love for the game out of his head or his heart. Once again, he signed with the Atlanta Falcons and once again, like every year, he had scheduling problems between the two teams. The Falcons let him play out the rest of the baseball season as long as he played for them on most Sundays, but when the Braves made the playoffs Deion found himself shuttling again, bringing on the incredible Sunday of October 11, when he played two sports in one day.

Deion was not a major factor in the Braves' baseball playoff success in 1992, but he was there and he did his best. He never abandoned the team. The Braves won the seventh and final game of the National League Championship Series to win the 1992 pennant and went on to play in the World Series, losing to the Toronto Blue Jays, 4 games to 2.

The end of the baseball season simply meant the start of the football season for Deion

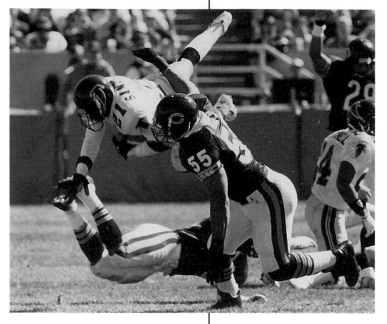

When Sanders cannot high step his way into the end zone, he will still try to sail for yardage on a kick or a punt return. His all-round play in 1992 earned him a trip to the Pro Bowl.

in 1992, and it was a football season to remember. The Falcons, like the Braves, were a poor football team in the late 1980s, languishing in last place or near it for several years. In 1989, the Falcons were so bad they drew just 7,792 fans to their final home game. They finished 1989 with a 3-13 record, their seventh consecutive losing season. Sanders's arrival helped the Falcons defense considerably, giving the offense time to build. The Falcons improved in 1990 and in 1991, with Sanders earning All Pro honors at cornerback, making it to the NFL playoffs for the first time in 10 years.

The 1992 season was a letdown for the Falcons but a good year for Deion. The Falcons, 10-6 in 1991, slumped all the way to 6-10 in 1992. Overall, it was an outstanding year for Sanders, the two-sport star. He finished among the top hitters in baseball and helped take his team to the World Series for a second time while earning All Pro honors in football.

By now he had become an "impact" player in football. Opposing players always looked to see where he was lining up at the start of each play—and they tried to keep the ball away from him. The fans, too, followed what Deion did on each down. It used to be that only offensive players had such an impact. Quarterbacks, running backs, and receivers were the fun people to watch, the guys who made the important plays. But the New York Giants' Lawrence Taylor showed that linebackers could be impact players too, and linemen such as Bruce Smith of the Buffalo Bills and Reggie White of the Philadelphia Eagles showed that they could control the field of play as well. Deion was the first to show that cornerback could be an impact role too. His opponents in the NFL never failed to praise Deion, even though they did not like his show-off style.

"On a one-play basis, he has got the ability to absolutely be the best in the NFL," said Redskins offensive coordinator Ron Lynn.

"He may be the fastest person I have ever seen on the football field," said Merton Hanks, a 49ers defensive back.

"He is as talented a guy as I've ever seen," said wide receiver Michael Irvin of the Dallas Cowboys. "Deion is a great corner. he is one of the best corners, if not the best corner, in the league. He has big games against big time players. You enjoy that."

Baseball people had nothing but praise for him.

"He always worked hard and had high goals. I knew he'd reach them," said Buck Showalter, manager of the Yankees, who was Sanders's skipper in the minor leagues.

Reggie Jackson, himself a controversial player in the 1970s, agreed. "Determination wins. Sanders has an amazing will to win and that's what makes him special," he said.

At long last, Deion Sanders had achieved all his dreams. He had become an all-star in both baseball and football, and at the same time.

6

GOOD TIMES AND BAD TIMES

Deion's sensational play for the Falcons in 1992 earned him a spot in the Pro Bowl. After the game, he shocked the press by announcing his retirement from pro football—again. He would now concentrate on baseball full-time.

"I'm tired," he said to reporters. "I've been driving myself too much. I'm 26 going on 36. I've lost the feeling—that excitement of playing football. I had no desire, no drive, no enthusiasm. I did notwant to be out there."

Sanders had talked about quitting football before, but in January 1993, he seemed to have his mind made up. He had finally chosen between the two sports after five long years. "There's so much in baseball that I want to do. I haven't attained the success I'm capable of, but I will this year. It might take a couple months or until midseason, but I'll do it," he said.

On April 22, Deion's father, just 50, died of a brain tumor. Deion was always very close to his mother, but Mims left home when Deion was

Sanders's return to baseball in 1993 was big news.

Sanders's speed on the basepaths greatly helped his team. In this 1992 game against the Florida Marlins, he just beat out a triple (as Gary Sheffield hopes for an out call). He would soon score on a balk.

young and the boy rarely saw him. Then, after Deion turned pro, he renewed his relationship with his father.

Deion took Mim's death very hard. He took four days off from the Braves to go to the funeral and be with his family. He was broken-hearted. He later began a ritual of hitting his chest and then looking up to the sky each time he scored or got a hit to honor his dad. The Braves had not renewed his contract and he felt the team did not want him. A week after his dad died, Deion, unhappy about everything, suddenly quit baseball.

Braves' general manager John Schuerholz talked to Sanders for weeks and offered him a three-year, $11-million contract. Deion accepted. He played just as well as he did in 1992, flirting with a .300 batting average through the spring and summer. He wound up hitting .276.

He also had an excellent season with the Atlanta Falcons in 1993, intercepting seven passes. It was a year, too, when many people began to change their minds about his showboat style of play. Many writers and fans objected to it when he came into sports because, with the exception of just a few (Joe Namath, say, or Muhammad Ali) most athletes were humble when they talked to the press and although many football players spiked footballs after touchdowns, none high stepped into the end zone so often and carried on the way Deion did.

Writers did not seem to mind that much, and neither did fans as the fall of 1993 wore on. Deion's teammates felt the same way. "He backs up everything he says on the field," said Bart Oates. "Most guys can't. As far as I'm concerned, the way he plays, he can talk all he wants."

Still, the Atlanta Braves became unhappy with Deion's style and his need to play football. They had three other excellent outfielders in Ron Gant, David Justice, and Otis Nixon, and so they traded him to the Cincinnati Reds.

"I'm happy," Deion said about his new life in Ohio. "I've got a great bunch of guys with me here. They want to win. These guys work hard, each and every one of them. They know what it takes to win. They know what it takes to be the best they can be. If everybody can be the best they can be individually, we're going to come out best, teamwise."

He impressed fans right away and continued to hit close to .300. Pitchers could not fool him. "With Deion, as a pitcher, you have to work so hard to get him out because you don't want him on first base," said hurler Jeff Brantley. "If he gets on first, it makes it so difficult to pitch to Barry Larkin and others because you're so worried about him."

Sanders was the first man in the batting cage and the last man out of it. He stole bases as well as anyone in the league. One time, he ran so fast after a hit that he slid into second for a double—on a grounder to the shortstop. An even better example of his will to win was the July 26 game against the Houston Astros.

Sanders ran from first to third on a hit by Barry Larkin and, thinking he could score, started running for home. The catcher blocked the plate and Deion lowered his shoulders and knocked him down and the ball out of his glove. He stood and stomped his right foot on the plate in joy as the crowd rose and cheered. Later, at his home, he received dozens of calls from his old football buddies who saw the crushing crash on television. "They asked me why I did not hit like that in football," Deion laughed.

In the middle of August 1994, *Baseball America* selected Deion as the number one baserunner in the National League and ranked him second as most exciting player (behind Barry Bonds). A midsummer slump pulled his average down a bit, to .283, but his 38 stolen bases were among the tops in the league, as were his 106 hits.

Sanders also saw Cincinnati as a city where he could again start organizations that would help inner-city kids. The president of Bank One, Emerson Brumback, was eager to develop a program for inner-city kids, too. The result was the Partnership for Kids and the Prime Time Youth Club, programs sponsored by the bank in which kids got free tickets to Reds baseball games, but only if they earned good grades in school or contributed to local community service groups.

The program was a great success. Deion spent considerable time with the kids and often brought groups of them on the field before games. He constantly told them to get an education, stay away from drugs and alcohol, and work hard. On the first day of a group visit, one boy, knowing how much money Deion made, stuck out his hand and said, "Give me five dollars!" Deion looked at him very seriously and then bent over to talk to him, eye to eye.

"I won't give you five dollars, but if you come back tomorrow I'll help you get a job where you can earn five dollars," he said.

He downplayed his flashy sports image, too, to remind kids that very few of them would ever become professional athletes but that all of them could work in the business community. To emphasize this, he turned down hundreds of life-size cardboard advertisements of himself in his Reds uniform for the program and posed instead in a business suit.

"Like many, I thought he was just a very flashy kind of athlete. He is not. He is a very serious man and he is very worried about the future of kids," said Bank One's marketing director, Bill Schumer.

"He sincerely wants to help our youth. He has come in and immediately let it be known that he will get involved with inner city communities, not only with black youth, but with all youth, and in all neighborhoods," said columnist James Clingman.

But Deion's Prime Time Kids club—and his latest season in the sun—stopped in August, when the long major league baseball strike began. It meant the end of the baseball season, but, strangely enough, it meant the beginning of an incredible journey for Deion Sanders.

Manager Davey Johnson of the Cincinatti Reds watches his new acquisition—a dynamic outfielder who can hit .300.

7

CALIFORNIA, HERE I COME: PLAYER OF THE YEAR

Deion Sanders found himself in a strange position in September of 1994. The strike shut down the baseball season in the middle of August and, after Labor Day, it appeared that there would be no more baseball for the rest of the year. He had made up his mind not to play football anymore back in the winter and the Falcons did not re-sign him. Deion had nowhere to play sports for the first time since he was seven years old.

His friends urged him to think about football again. Sanders spent three weeks visiting different teams and their coaches and going to stadiums to see games. He was pursued by everybody. New Orleans offered $17 million for four years. Miami also wanted to make him a multi-millionaire. He stunned everyone by picking the San Francisco 49ers—at just $1.1 million for a year—under one of the most unusual

Sanders was still playing for the Reds when he played his first game for the San Francisco 49ers in 1994. Here he sports his trademark kerchief.

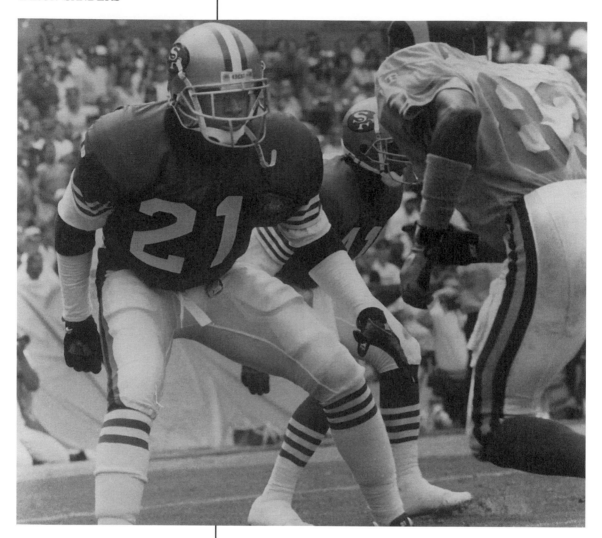

The 49ers added a lot of high-priced talent before the start of their 1994 season. But none had an impact equal to that of their star cornerback.

agreements in sports history. Deion would become their defensive back and punt and kick-off returner, but only for the rest of the 1994 season. Deion wanted a home while the baseball strike lasted and the 49ers saw in him the key to their first Super Bowl in five years. It was a good match. He could come back to San Francisco the following year if he wanted to, or he could re-sign with some other team. Deion could also play baseball all of 1995 if he wanted. There were no obligations for anybody and Deion could concentrate on just one sport for the first time in his life after years of being torn between two. He felt a great sense of relief.

But why turn down far richer deals to play in San Francisco? The answer was simple, said Deion, "I'm going to win the Super Bowl with San Francisco." Of course, it did not hurt that by joining a high-profile team like the 49ers, Sanders's endorsement deals were much more valuable. He had a lucrative deal with a sneaker company and several other sponsors—and they were all happy to see him playing for a team that would get national exposure week in and week out. The 49ers were in the process of putting together an astonishing roster. They already featured such stars as Steve Young and Jerry Rice. Now they had also added Bart Oates, Ken Norton, Jr., and Ricky Jackson.

San Francisco newspapers carried stories about "Neon Deion" and his nonstop talking, dollar-sign underpants, gold chains, and showboating. Some writers wondered whether Deion was too wild for the rather quiet 49ers, whether he would upset "team chemistry." Other writers were glad to see him in a 49ers uniform. "This is the most dangerous cornerback in football, folks, possibly the best kick return man in pads, and the most entertaining defensive guy alive, on and off the field. Sanders will be a hand grenade with legs," wrote Scott Ostler in the *San Francisco Chronicle*.

Deion went to the other players the very first day he arrived and told them that no matter how much he did or did not play, he wanted them to be friends and to be a team together. He wanted to be just another player and would play his heart out for them. They were impressed.

"We had all heard a lot about Deion and his style and you wonder about a guy like that," said Bart Oates, a 49ers lineman. He was very different, though. In just a few days, we could see that the gold chains and talk were just for entertainment. Underneath all that, he was quite a nice guy. I never saw anybody who worked so hard. He truly wanted us to go to the Super Bowl and he worked like a dog all year to be the best defensive back in football. It was never an individual thing for him. He always played for the team. The guys admired Deion very much."

Around the NFL, everybody sensed something special from Sanders at San Francisco. "He has revolutionized the game," said Joe Vitt, Rams assistant coach. "He shuts down your receiver. You're defending against 10, not 11, because Deion's man is off the board. he is no longer a factor in the game. When you take Deion and put him on the opponent's best receiver and shut him down, now you've shut down the capabilities of that offense 40 to 50 per cent. he is the best cornerback. You make training reels up trying to teach your people to play like this guy. he is that good."

The 49ers struggled during their first few games, but when Deion arrived their fortunes turned around. His first start was against the New Orleans Saints. The 49ers held a 17–13 lead with less than a minute left. New Orleans filled the air with passes in a desperate attempt to score. Suddenly, out of nowhere, Deion Sanders intercepted a pass at the San Francisco 24 yardline and raced up the field for a 76-yard

touchdown, high stepping and showboating the last 30 yards as only Neon Deion could. The crowd roared.

That sensational interception, and the high stepping, signaled the start of an incredible season for both Deion and the 49ers. "In approximately 87 electrifying strides, Sanders turned the dullest afternoon at Candlestick Park . . .

The 49ers were feeling so good about the progress of the Super Bowl that late in the game they inserted Deion on offense. Steve Young threw a pass to Deion, but Stanley Richards of the San Diego Chargers broke it up.

into a standing, stomping, Prime Time carnival yesterday," wrote columnist C. W. Nevius in the *San Francisco Chronicle*.

An even bigger moment came on October 16, when he flew with the 49ers to Atlanta to play the Falcons, the team that let him go. Deion was determined to get revenge somehow, especially after fans booed him, and midway through the first half he got his chance. Falcons quarterback Jeff George tried to hit a receiver near the goal line, but Deion stepped in front of the receiver at the 7 and picked off the ball. As he began to race straight down the sideline for what would be a 93-yard touchdown, he realized it was the Atlanta sideline. He ran sideways, pointing at his former teammates and carrying on a whole conversation as he ran by them. Then, with 40 yards to go, he looked up at the fans and began his patented high stepping, which he did all the way into the end zone, where he did a dance. It was pure Deion and 49ers fans loved it.

What counted the most, though, was that Deion was helping the 49ers win. His touchdown at New Orleans preserved a win and his touchdown in Atlanta gave the 49ers a 6–3 lead, which they built on for another win, making them 5-2. A few weeks later, against the Rams, Deion knocked down a pass in the end zone that appeared to a sure touchdown to save a 31–27 win for the 49ers. San Francisco began to win again and again, with number 21 in the secondary, and by the end of the season players and fans believed they had a chance to go all the way to the Super Bowl. Deion had a new fan club, too—his teammates. "From the day he arrived, all he wanted to do was do his part. Everybody liked Deion. He is such a likable guy . . . He came in here, he knew everybody thought he'd be something outlandish, and everybody was so relieved that he is so down to earth," said safety Tim McDonald.

At the end of the season, Deion was voted the NFL's Defensive Player of the Year in a landslide by the same sportswriters who were so critical of him at its start. He won the award even though he did not run back kickoffs or punts for the 49ers (they already had Dexter Carter for those chores).

Deion appreciated it all, but he had other things on his mind, such as a Super Bowl ring.

He wanted to go to the Super Bowl to give his team a chance to win the world championship, but he had a personal goal, too. No one in the history of sports had ever played in a World Series and a Super Bowl. Deion, who played in the World Series with the Braves in 1991 and 1992, wanted to be the first.

Before the 49ers could get to the Super Bowl in Miami, they had to get past the Dallas Cowboys in the NFC championship game. The Cowboys had won the previous two Super Bowls and had a strong chance to become the first team ever to win three in a row. Sports commentators said the Cowboys were going to be the toughest opponent of the year for San Francisco.

They were. The Cowboys, with running back Emmitt Smith, quarterback Troy Aikman, and wide receiver Michael Irvin, were a good team. The 49ers were better, though, and in a hardfought game they beat the Cowboys, ending their chances for three straight Super Bowls. Then it was on to Miami. The 49ers, playing better in the playoffs than they did all year, were expected to crush the San Diego Chargers, and they did. Steve Young and Jerry Rice hooked up for a touchdown on the third play from scrimmage— the fastest TD in Super Bowl history—and the 49ers piled on more points soon after. The very end of the game turned out to be one of Deion Sanders's finest moments, showcasing all of his skills and personality in a single play. The Chargers moved into 49ers territory with less than a minute to play. A possible touchdown pass was deflected at the line and knocked high into the air. Sanders, covering his man in the end zone, saw it pop high up into the sky out of the corner of his eye. He moved over, then up towards the goal line and intercepted the ball as it came down. He cut left, then right and looked up the field. In his mind he saw himself running 102 yards for a touchdown. He made it up to his own 22 yardline before he was tackled. The Charger who tackled him, frustrated, started shouting at Deion. Sanders stood up, pulled off his helmet and, his red kerchief tied tight around his head, pointed up at the scoreboard, which showed a 49er victory. That one moment said it all.

Neon Deion had done it. He not only became the first player to ever play in the World Series and Super Bowl, but he even intercepted a pass in the Super Bowl.

Sanders's future may not include a whole lot more football and baseball. In the summer of 1995, after being traded from the Reds to the San Francisco Giants, he was once again uncertain which direction his career would take. Regardless, he has accomplished more in two sports than most athletes ever accomplish in one.

CHRONOLOGY

1967   Deion Sanders is born.

1985   Accepts scholarship to play football at Florida State University, learns how to play cornerback after having been a quarterback in high school.

1987   Wins All-American honors in football; helps lead FSU to victory in Fiesta Bowl; also stars in collegiate football.

1988   Again wins All-American honors in football; helps lead FSU to victory in Sugar Bowl.

1989   Drafted by the New York Yankees to play baseball; also drafted by the Atlanta Falcons to play football. Signs an $11.2 million contract with the Falcons. Returns kicks and plays outstanding defense; is named an All Pro.

1990   Again named All Pro; Falcons make the playoffs for first time in 10 years.

1991   Joins the Atlanta Braves; plays in the World Series against the Minnesota Twins.

1992   Bats .304 for the Braves; again plays in the World Series. Also plays in Football's Pro Bowl.

1993   Signs $11 million contract with Atlanta Braves who then trade Sanders to the Cincinnati Reds.

1994   Joins San Francisco 49ers and helps them win the Super Bowl. In so doing, Sanders becomes first athlete ever to play in both a Super Bowl and World Series.

1995   Traded from the Cincinnati Reds to the San Francisco Giants.

STATISTICS

DEION SANDERS

BASEBALL

YEAR	TEAM	G	R	H	HR	RBI	AVE	SB
1989	Yankees	14	7	11	2	7	.234	1
1990	Yankees	57	24	21	3	9	.158	8
1991	Braves	54	16	21	4	13	.191	11
1992	Braves	97	54	92	8	28	.304	26
1993	Braves	95	42	75	6	28	.276	19
1994	Braves/Reds	92	48	106	4	28	.283	38
TOTALS		409	191	326	27	113	.264	103

FOOTBALL

| Year | Team | G | PUNT RETURNS | | | KICKOFF RETURNS | | | |
			INT	NO	AVE	NO	AVE	PC	TD
1989	Atlanta	15	5	28	11.0	35	20.7	1	1
1990	Atlanta	16	3	29	8.6	39	21.8	0	3
1991	Atlanta	15	6	21	8.1	26	22.2	1	2
1992	Atlanta	13	3	13	3.2	40	26.7	3	3
1993	Atlanta	11	7	2	10.5	7	24.1	6	1
1994	San Francisco	16	8	0	0	1	25	0	3
TOTALS		86	32	93	8.5	148	23.1	11	13

G	games	INT	interceptions
R	runs	NO	number
H	hits	PC	passes caught
HR	home runs	TD	touchdowns
RBI	runs batted in		
AVE	average		
SB	stolen bases		

SUGGESTIONS FOR FURTHER READING

Hinton, Ed. "One Thing...Or the Other." *Sports Illustrated*, April 27, 1992.

King, Peter. "Time for a Game Plan." *Sports Illustrated*, July 8, 1992.

Kirkpatrick, Curry. "A Player Who's Always On." *Newsweek*, November 7, 1994.

Lupica, Mike. "The Neon Nineties." *Esquire*, June 1992.

Parker, Rob. "Double Play." *YSB Magazine*, September 1993.

Weinberg, Rick. "Deion Sanders: Interview." *Sport*, July 1994.'

ABOUT THE AUTHOR

Bruce Chadwick, a longtime columnist with the New York Daily News, has written over 300 magazine articles, 12 nonfiction books, and one novel. Among his books are *When the Game was Black and White, American Summers: Minor League Baseball,* and *Joe Namath* for Chelsea House's "Football Legends" series. Chadwick teaches writing at New York University and is an associate resident fellow at the Smithsonian, where he lectures on baseball's role in American society.

INDEX

PICTURE CREDITS
AP/Wide World Photos: 2, 8, 11, 12, 22, 24, 30, 32, 35, 36, 39, 42, 46, 52, 57; Tom Price: 16, 18; UPI/Bettmann: 48, 51; Courtesy San Francisco 49ers: 54.